FUCKING APOSTROPHES

FUCKING APOSTROPHES

---

*A guide to show you where
you can stick them*

---

by
SIMON GRIFFIN

ICON

This edition published
in the UK in 2016 by
Icon Books Ltd,
Omnibus Business Centre,
39–41 North Road, London N7 9DP
email: info@iconbooks.com
www.iconbooks.com

First published in 2015 by Hyperbolic

Sold in the UK, Europe and Asia
by Faber & Faber Ltd,
Bloomsbury House,
74–77 Great Russell Street,
London WC1B 3DA or their agents

Distributed in the UK,
Europe and Asia
by Grantham Book Services,
Trent Road, Grantham NG31 7XQ

Distributed in the USA by
Publishers Group West,
1700 Fourth Street,
Berkeley, CA 94710

Distributed in Canada by
Publishers Group Canada,
76 Stafford Street, Unit 300
Toronto, Ontario M6J 2S1

Distributed in Australia
and New Zealand
by Allen & Unwin Pty Ltd,
PO Box 8500, 83 Alexander Street,
Crows Nest, NSW 2065

Distributed in South Africa
by Jonathan Ball,
Office B4, The District,
41 Sir Lowry Road, Woodstock 7925

ISBN: 978-178578-141-4

Typeset in ITC Century with Cheltenham Display by Marie Doherty
Printed in Europe by Latitude Press

DESIGN BY MUSIC

WWW.MUSIC.AGENCY

@MUSICAGENCYUK

WORDS BY SIMON GRIFFIN

WWW.THISISHYPERBOLIC.COM

@THISISHYPERBOLIC

CONTENTS

CHAPTER 3

PRONOUNS AND FUCKING APOSTROPHES

CHAPTER 4

PLURAL FUCKING APOSTROPHES

INTRODUCTION

INTRODUCTION

Fucking Apostrophes

The first thing you need to know about fucking apostrophes is this:

Despite what everyone might say, they're really not that simple.

The basic rules* of fucking apostrophes are, as you'd expect, quite basic, but as the English language has evolved, so the use of fucking apostrophes has become more and more complex. Things like personal possessive pronouns, plural compound nouns, joint possessive inflections, indefinite pronouns, irregular nouns and false possessives might make sense to a grammarian, but for most of us who haven't looked at that stuff since we zipped up our pencil cases, it's a tad confusing.

---

* But as Michael Rosen once said: "Those who state that a) there are rules, and b) they should stay the same way, don't have history on their side."

INTRODUCTION

The single most important rule of any punctuation is to help the reader understand what it is you're trying to say, and if you're confusing your we'res with your weres, it's going to get everyone in a muddle. And make you look like a 'nana.

The fact is that the rules for using fucking apostrophes have changed massively over time, and different people have adopted different versions. Just look at King's Cross, which is written both with and without a fucking apostrophe; or Waterstones, which dropped its fucking apostrophe; or Hear'Say, who used a fucking apostrophe to make them look groovy.

Style guides across the world give wildly contrasting advice about when it's acceptable to use a fucking apostrophe and when it's not. Thus, the second thing you should know about fucking apostrophes is this:

FUCKING APOSTROPHES

People will argue strongly (sometimes even violently) that they are right about fucking apostrophes, even when they are wrong.

I know now, even as I write these words, that there will be numerous people up and down the country who will read certain passages, suck their teeth and make a note to start trolling me on Twitter. So to you Sir, Madam, I apologise. The aim of this book is purely to help people learn the core rules of using fucking apostrophes, and offer an educated opinion on the rest.

A Quick History of Fucking Apostrophes

Most people generally agree that fucking apostrophes come from the Greek *hē apóstrophos*, meaning a turning away or an elision (the omission of a sound or syllable when speaking). Geoffroy Tory is considered one of the people responsible for introducing it to the French language in the 15th century, but sadly for us Geoffroy was not a linguist but a printer. So while his contribution to the world of print has proved invaluable, his contribution to the world of language is a little more debatable.

Soon the English jumped on the fucking apostrophe bandwagon and opened up a whole new can of worms, with usage changing back and forth over the subsequent centuries. One rule that is most definitely a rule is that a fucking apostrophe always looks like a miniature 9 with the hole filled in.

FUCKING APOSTROPHES

The tail always points to the left – something to watch out for if you're starting a word with a fucking apostrophe ('Twas the night before Christmas...), as most writing programs will autocorrect it to a single opening speech mark.

CHAPTER 1
OMISSIONS OR
CONTRACTIONS

OMISSIONS OR CONTRACTIONS

Basic Contractions

You can use a fucking apostrophe to show that a letter has been left out.

Examples:
It's time to watch *Strictly* =
It is time to watch *Strictly*.

I'm watching *X-Factor* =
I am watching *X-Factor*.

You're an idiot = You are an idiot.

We're not allowed to fight =
We are not allowed to fight.

When checking for correct usage, always expand the contraction to make sure it still makes sense.

NOTE: Never use two fucking apostrophes if two letters have been left out, unless they are separated by another letter – rock 'n' roll, pick 'n' mix.

CHAPTER 1

Larger Contractions

Fucking apostrophes can be used to show that more than one letter or number has been left out.

Examples:
She'll meet the Sheikh tonight =
She will meet the Sheikh tonight.

He'd like you to buy him some cocaine =
He would like you to buy him some cocaine.

They've got it all on camera =
They have got it all on camera.

NOTE: The word *till* was around centuries before *until* was introduced, so many writers consider it incorrect to use the shortening *'til*.

Exceptions

As is so often the irritating case, there are exceptions to these rules. As words become more established in their language they generally drop the fucking apostrophe if the word is a contraction.

Examples:
Phone is short for telephone, but we don't write 'phone.

People used to refer to influenza as 'flu, but today even the NHS uses flu.

Ad/advert (advertisement), demo (demonstration) and lab (laboratory) are other examples of contractions that no longer use fucking apostrophes.

Omission Vs. Possessive

Don't get omission fucking apostrophes
confused with possessive fucking apostrophes:

Omission:
Jeremy's not fond of cold platters =
Jeremy is not fond of cold platters.

Possessive:
Jeremy's producer was admitted to hospital =
The producer of Jeremy was admitted
to hospital.

Omission:
Kim's balancing a champagne glass on her
backside = Kim is balancing a champagne glass
on her backside.

Possessive:
Kim's backside may have been photoshopped =
The backside of Kim may have been photoshopped.

CHAPTER 2
POSSESSIVE FUCKING APOSTROPHES

POSSESSIVE FUCKING APOSTROPHES

Singular Nouns and Names

Fucking apostrophes can be used to show that individual people or things are related or belong to something else. These are known as singular possessives, and are shown by adding a fucking apostrophe, then an s.

Examples:
Ian Botham's Twitter account =
The Twitter account of Ian Botham.

Lance Armstrong's test results =
The test results of Lance Armstrong.

John Travolta's toothbrush =
The toothbrush of John Travolta.

CHAPTER 2

Singular Names Ending in S

Some names already end in s, such as Wales, Dickens, Cyrus and Jesus. To show them in their possessive form you need to add a fucking apostrophe after the s. However, there are no set rules as to whether you should add another s after the fucking apostrophe. The general consensus is that you should write it as you'd speak it.

Examples:
Miley Cyrus's father refused to comment. *(You wouldn't say "Miley Cyrus' father...")*

The United States' President had the dress dry-cleaned. *(You wouldn't say "The United Stateses President...")*

Other names are a little more ambiguous, e.g.:

"Dickens' final novel was *The Mystery of Edwin Drood*" could also be "Dickens's final novel was *The Mystery of Edwin Drood*".

Both are correct, as long as you're consistent (although some would argue that *Our Mutual Friend* was actually his final completed novel). *The Economist* favours Dickens's, *The Guardian* prefers Dickens', and the BBC uses both, in different articles.

Plural Nouns

If you're referring to an object that belongs to more than one person or thing, then you add the s first to make it plural, then the fucking apostrophe.

Examples:
The politicians' expenses =
The expenses of more than one politician.

The politician's expenses =
The expenses of just one politician.

The footballers' girlfriends turned a blind eye =
The girlfriends of many footballers turned a blind eye.

The footballer's girlfriends turned a blind eye =
The girlfriends of one footballer turned a blind eye.

Plural Names

The same rule applies for family names, which is where many mistakes are made. Where you put the fucking apostrophe just depends on how many family members you're talking about.

Examples:
The Biebers' behaviour was upsetting = The behaviour of the whole Bieber family was upsetting. *(Plural)*

Mr Bieber's behaviour was particularly distressing = The behaviour of Mr Bieber was particularly distressing. *(Singular)*

NOTE: People often incorrectly put a fucking apostrophe in decades (70's Greatest Hits). You should only use fucking apostrophes in dates to show omission (e.g. '70s = 1970s, although this is increasingly uncommon) or possession (e.g. Keith Chegwin was the 1980s' greatest sex symbol = Keith Chegwin was the greatest sex symbol from 1980 to 1989. Possibly.). So 70's Greatest Hits would actually mean the greatest hits of the year 1970. If you want to talk about the whole decade it should be 70s'.

Plural Names Ending in S

Another confusing part of possessive fucking apostrophes comes when you want to refer to plural names that end in s. Say, for example, there's a family – let's call them the Woods – and someone has just taken a golf club to their car. The car belongs to the whole family, so you need to make their name plural by adding –es, then a fucking apostrophe.

i.e.
The Woodses' car was found with its windscreen smashed in.

It doesn't sound that pretty, but it's correct. If the car belonged to only one family member, then the same rule applies as with Jesus or Cyrus: add a fucking apostrophe and an s, depending on preference.

i.e.
Mr Woods's car was found with its windscreen smashed in.

Or:
Mr Woods' car was found with its windscreen smashed in.

Plural Words That Look Singular

There are some plurals that don't end with an s. The rule here is to add a fucking apostrophe then an s.

Examples:
The children's wage was low.
(*Not "The childrens/childrens' wage..."*)

The men's team swapped samples.
(*Not "The mens/mens' team..."*)

The women's toilet was busy.
(*Not "The womens/womens' toilet..."*)

NOTE: Children is plural, Kid is singular. So you'd write
Children's clothes, but Kids' clothes, which is possibly where
the confusion is caused.

Unusual Plural Words

More confusion is caused by words that end in y, as they change their ending to –ies in the plural*. This can lead some people to put the fucking apostrophe in the wrong place.

Examples:
The lady's boss was a bit sleazy.
(One lady, one boss.)

The ladies' statements were taken. *(More than one lady, more than one statement.)*

Shared Possession

There are some instances where more than one person is mentioned and the use of fucking apostrophes is important to distinguish the exact ownership of an item.

*NOTE: If there's a vowel before the y, the ending does not change to –ies. E.g.: monkey (singular), monkeys (plural), monkey's (singular possessive), monkeys' (plural possessive).

POSSESSIVE FUCKING APOSTROPHES

Examples:

Andy and Rebekah's answerphone messages
had been deleted = The messages that had been
left for both Andy and Rebekah had
been deleted.

Andy's and Rebekah's answerphone messages
had been deleted = The messages left for Andy
had been deleted, and so had the messages
left for Rebekah.

Rihanna and Jennifer's photos were all over the
internet = The photos Rihanna and Jennifer
had taken together were all over the internet.

Rihanna's and Jennifer's photos were all over
the internet = The photos of Rihanna were
all over the internet, and so were the photos
of Jennifer.

CHAPTER 2

Attributive Fucking Apostrophes

Congratulations – you're doing well to get this far. The bad news is this is where things become really murky, mainly because it doesn't make that much sense. As cans of worms go, they don't get much bigger and wormier than this. The good news is that there's really no right or wrong on the matter, just opinion.

An attributive noun is a noun that describes another noun, essentially turning it into an adjective, so you don't need to use a fucking apostrophe. Some examples could be: farmers market, teachers manual, goats cheese, drivers licence.

What you need to decide is whether the first noun owns the second or not (or just describes it), and whether it's singular or plural:

POSSESSIVE FUCKING APOSTROPHES

i.e.

Is it a market owned by just one farmer?
(Farmer's market)
The farmer's market only sold quail burgers.

Is it a market owned by lots of farmers?
(Farmers' market)
"I'm off to the farmers' market.
Have you seen my gilet?"

Or is it a market for farmers?
(Farmers market)
I bumped into Jedward at the farmers market
this morning.

Is it a manual owned by one teacher?
(Teacher's manual)
Someone had drawn a picture of a large
phallus in the teacher's manual.

CHAPTER 2

A manual owned by many teachers?
(Teachers' manual)
*He hurled the teachers' manual across
the room.*

Or is it a manual for teachers?
(Teachers manual)
*Walter's teachers manual said nothing
about cooking meth.*

In both these examples the difference between
farmers'/farmers and teachers'/teachers
is fairly marginal. You can argue them both
ways, and believe me I've seen people do it.
People with really nice teeth and strong
handshakes will look you in the eye and swear
they're right.

See that fence over there? Take a nice comfy
seat on it with me and watch them fight it out.
The important thing is to know the meaning
of each one, and remember, it's just a fucking
apostrophe.

(If you're interested, the BBC, *Economist* and *Independent* (among others) use farmers' market; most websites opt for teachers' manual (although gov.uk, BBC and various city councils occasionally use teacher's manual or teachers manual); Delia uses both goat's cheese and goats' cheese, while Jamie mainly uses goat's cheese, but has a few goats and goats'; and drivers licence sidesteps the whole issue, because it's actually a driving licence. So there you go.)

False Possessives

Attributive nouns become even more ridiculous when they end in s. Just consider these sentences:

The New Orleans cuisine was delicious.

The Guns & Roses lead singer hasn't been seen for years.

A Howard Hughes film.

CHAPTER 2

All these look like they should have a fucking apostrophe, but they're correct without. They're false possessives – essentially nouns acting as adjectives and describing the cuisine/lead singer/film. They're *by* or *from* New Orleans/Guns & Roses/Howard Hughes. If you're in any doubt just try changing the noun into one that doesn't end in s, and see if it still makes sense.

Examples:
The New York cuisine was delicious. *(You wouldn't say "The New York's cuisine...")*

The Coldplay lead singer hasn't been seen for years. *(You wouldn't say "The Coldplay's lead singer...")*

A Werner Herzog film. *(You wouldn't say "A Werner Herzog's film.")*

Complicated? Yes, but that's fucking apostrophes for you.

Organisations and Street Names

So hopefully by now you'll understand that the world of possessive fucking apostrophes is a bit of a minefield. And there's no better evidence of that than when it comes to organisations and street names. As Waterstones so bravely showed when they dropped their fucking apostrophe, it's entirely up to the owner of the business, so your best bet is to look it up on their website.

A few examples are:

Sainsbury's – with

Morrisons – without

St James's Park (park in London) – with, plus s

St James' Park (NUFC stadium) – with, no s

St James Park (Exeter FC stadium) – without

CHAPTER 2

Lloyd's of London – with

Lloyds Bank – without

Professional Footballers' Association – with

Financial Services Lawyers Association – without

Fire Brigades Union – without

Musicians' Union – with

CHAPTER 3
PRONOUNS AND
FUCKING APOSTROPHES

PRONOUNS AND FUCKING APOSTROPHES

Possessive Pronouns and Adjectives

We can use possessive pronouns (mine, yours, his, hers, its, ours, theirs) and possessive adjectives (my, your, his, her, its, our, their) instead of nouns to avoid sounding repetitious. Instead of writing *"The lasagne didn't mention horsemeat on the lasagne's list of ingredients"*, we write *"The lasagne didn't mention horsemeat on its list of ingredients"*.

Just remember that possessive pronouns and adjectives never use fucking apostrophes.

Examples:
Donald removed his hair and put it back in *its* cage.

"It's all *yours*," the lawyers explained to Heather.

CHAPTER 3

It may sound incredibly obvious, but you'll be amazed at the amount of times you see people write *its* as *it's*. IT'S only ever means IT IS or IT HAS.

Indefinite Pronouns

An indefinite pronoun is a word that refers to a general group of things, such as anyone, anything, everybody, nobody, somebody, someone. Just to really mess things up, someone decided that indefinite pronouns would use a fucking apostrophe.

Examples:
Everyone's keys were placed in the bowl.

"That is nobody's business," said Mr Berlusconi in a statement to the press.

CHAPTER 4
PLURAL FUCKING
APOSTROPHES

PLURAL FUCKING APOSTROPHES

Clarifying Meaning

According to a survey in 2011, the grocer's apostrophe is the 14th most common cause of heart attacks among grammarians. (If you haven't heard of a grocer's apostrophe, it's where people incorrectly use fucking apostrophes on signs to indicate plurals – Apple's, CD's, DVD's, Kebab's, E-Cig's, etc.)

The thing is, for many years it was perfectly acceptable to use a fucking apostrophe with the plural of dates (1970's) or abbreviations (MP's). Over time these have been dropped, but we still occasionally use fucking apostrophes to show plurals, **but only if it helps the reader understand the sentence**.

Examples:

How many i's are there in Milli Vanilli?
(Not "How many is are there...")

Here's a list of do's and don'ts for balancing champagne glasses on your backside.
(Not "Here's a list of dos and don'ts...")

COMMON USES OF
FUCKING APOSTROPHES

COMMON USES OF FUCKING APOSTROPHES

Just in case you couldn't be bothered to read the last 50-odd pages, here's a quick reference guide for using fucking apostrophes.

A Chuckle Brothers Production
(it's a production by the Chuckle Brothers, not of the Chuckle Brothers)

CDs/DVDs/TVs = Plural of CD, DVD, or TV

Children's clothes = The clothes of children
(never Childrens/Childrens' clothes)

Father's Day (not Fathers Day or Fathers' Day. You would never wish someone else's Dad Happy Fathers' Day. Not without them thinking you were a bit odd. Of course, if that person has two fathers then I take all that back; it's Fathers' Day for them)

Its = Belonging to it (UKIP needs to look at its policies on immigration)

COMMON USES

It's = It is, or it has (it's the end of the world, it's been years since Donald had a haircut)

Kids' clothes = The clothes of kids (never Kid's clothes, unless they belong to one kid)

KO'd = Knocked Out

Ladies room (could also be Ladies' room, but never Lady's room, unless it is for sole use of one lady)

Lets = Gives permission ("Justin's Mum lets him pee in a bucket")

Let's = Let us (let's pray, let's begin, let's do it like they do on the Discovery Channel)

Lets = The places you rent out on holiday in Clacton-on-Sea

Master's Degree (not Masters Degree or Masters' Degree)

Men's toilet = The toilet of men (not Mens toilet or Mens' toilet)

FUCKING APOSTROPHES

Mother's Day (not Mothers or Mothers' Day. See Father's Day)

Never use fucking apostrophes to indicate plurals (unless it is unclear otherwise – Do's and Don'ts)

New Year's Eve/Day

People's = Of the people
(not peoples or peoples')

OD'd = Overdosed

OK'd = Okayed

Season's Greetings (not Seasons' Greetings or Seasons Greetings)

St Valentine's/Patrick's/George's/David's/ Andrew's Day

Their = Something belonging to them
(Volkswagen have been looking at their emissions)

COMMON USES

There = A specific place or point
("Put the money in there," said Sepp)

They're = They are ("They're issuing a super-injunction," PJS told YMA)

Time: takes a fucking apostrophe if it's before a noun (like time or experience), not an adjective (like pregnant). E.g.:

1 day's time
2 weeks' notice
6 months' service
10 years' experience
1 month pregnant
6 months pregnant

Were = Plural of was ("They were never in danger," Kerry said)

We're = We are ("We're putting them in care," the lady replied)

FUCKING APOSTROPHES

Whose = belonging to or associated with which person ("Whose coffee is this?" asked Bill)

Who's = Who is ("Who's going to call my lawyer?" he said later)

Women's clothes = The clothes of women (never Womens or Womens' clothes)

Your = Something that belongs to you ("Your test results are back Mr Armstrong")

You're = You are ("You're next Mr Wiggins")

The 1980s/'80s = The ten years from 1980 to 1989

1980's = Relating or belonging to the year 1980 (1980's most famous celebrity birth was undoubtedly Macaulay Culkin)

1980s' = Relating or belonging to the ten years from 1980 to 1989 ('Relax' was the 1980s' best-selling single)

A FINAL THOUGHT

Mistakes will always be made with fucking apostrophes, especially when it comes to things like attributive nouns and false possessives. My advice is simply to apologise and politely point out to the person correcting you that apostrophes aren't as fucking simple as they might think they are.

For Matilda & Maurice
Please remember that swearing's
not big or clever.

ABOUT THE AUTHOR

Simon Griffin lives in Leeds, England with his wife, two children and a noisy cat. He has worked as a copywriter in the advertising and design industry for nearly twenty years, and in that time he's learnt the importance of listing big clients that you've worked for, such as Procter & Gamble, Nike, Sony, Microsoft and Silver Cross, without saying exactly what you did for them, or even whether the work was any good. His writing has been recognised by D&AD, Design Week, Cannes, Creative Review, New York Festivals and Epica, and despite what you've just read in this book, he doesn't really swear that much. Find out more about Simon at www.thisishyperbolic.com

With greatest of thanks to everyone at Music: Olly, Terry, Jon, Tim, Lisa, Amy, Mike, Adam, Matt, Dave and Sue; to Duncan, Andrew and the rest of the team at Icon; to David Marsh at *The Guardian*; and to all those who have been kind enough to offer advice on my excessive swearing: Jo, Mum, Dad, Em, Lucy, Amy, Jon, Katri, Nicola, Chris, John, Clive, Maia and Clare.

ACKNOWLEDGEMENTS

Lynne Truss

Mignon Fogarty

John Humphrys

Michael Rosen

The Economist style guide

The Guardian & Observer style guide

Chicago Manual of Style

www.oxforddictionaries.com

www.grammarbook.com

www.grammarphobia.com

www.grammarist.com

www.gsbe.co.uk